Yikes! Wow! Yuck!

Yikes! Wow! Yuck!

Fun Experiments for Your First Science Fair

Elizabeth Snoke Harris

Illustrated by Nora Thompson

LARK BOOKS

A Division of Sterling Publishing Co., Inc.
New York / London

Editor: Rain Newcomb
Creative Director & Cover Design: Celia Naranjo
Art Director: Robin Gregory
Art Production Assistant: Bradley Norris
Editorial Assistance: Rose McLarney and Cassie Moore
Illustrator: Nora Thompson

Library of Congress Cataloging-in-Publication Data

Harris, Elizabeth Snoke, 1973-
  Yikes! wow! yuck! : fun experiments for your first science fair / by
Elizabeth Snoke Harris ; illustrated by Nora Thompson.
       p. cm.
  Includes index.
  ISBN-13: 978-1-57990-930-7 (hc-plc with jacket : alk. paper)
  ISBN-10: 1-57990-930-2 (hc-plc with jacket : alk. paper)
  1. Science projects-Juvenile literature. 2.
Science--Experiments--Juvenile literature. I. Thompson, Nora. II. Title.
  Q182.3.H379 2008
  507.8--dc22

                                        2007019770

10 9 8 7 6 5 4 3 2

Published by Lark Books, A Division of Sterling Publishing Co., Inc.
387 Park Avenue South, New York, N.Y. 10016

Text © 2008, Elizabeth Snoke Harris
Illustrations © 2008, Nora Thompson

Distributed in Canada by Sterling Publishing, c/o Canadian Manda Group, 165 Dufferin Street
Toronto, Ontario, Canada M6K 3H6

Distributed in the United Kingdom by GMC Distribution Services,
Castle Place, 166 High Street, Lewes, East Sussex, England BN7 1XU

Distributed in Australia by Capricorn Link (Australia) Pty Ltd.,
P.O. Box 704, Windsor, NSW 2756 Australia

If you have questions or comments about this book, please contact:
Lark Books, 67 Broadway, Asheville, NC 28801, (828) 253-0467

Manufactured in China

ISBN 13: 978-1-57990-930-7

For information about custom editions, special sales, premium and corporate
purchases, please contact Sterling Special Sales Department at 800-805-5489
or specialsales@sterlingpub.com.

Contents

It's Science Fair Time!

Are you ready to do your first science fair experiment? You don't need to wear a lab coat or goggles to do your experiment—unless you really want to. When you're done, you'll show off your science smarts to your family, friends, teachers, and judges at the fair. If this sounds a little scary, don't worry—this book will make it all easy and fun!

What's a Science Fair Experiment?

A science fair experiment gives you the chance to explore something that interests you. You're going to figure out why something works the way it does. Here's a secret: you already do this—without even trying—every day. You experiment with balance when you ride your bike. When you play catch, you learn how things fly through the air and how to make them go where you want.

The only difference between your science fair experiment and what you do every day is that you're going to follow a plan called the *scientific method*. This book will help you with every step, from coming up with an idea to presenting what you learned.

How to Choose an Experiment

First, get a notebook to write notes in. Ask your teacher for a copy of the science fair rules. Then look through this book. It's full of ideas for experiments about everything, from knocking over dominos to exploding soda—and even some stinky stuff. Choose one that looks interesting. Read through the entire experiment. Then ask yourself three questions:

- Am I interested in finding out what happens?
- Can I get all the materials I need?
- Do I have enough time to do all the steps carefully and completely?

If you answered "yes" to every question, you've found your science fair experiment! Write down what it is and the reasons you chose it in your notebook.

The Scientific Method

The scientific method is a plan that scientists use to help them answer questions. All of the experiments in this book will help you follow the scientific method. There are five steps:

1. Ask a Question
2. Research the Question
3. Choose a Hypothesis
4. Do the Experiment
5. Draw a Conclusion

Research It

You need to learn more about your topic, which means doing research. Here's what you do:

- Find at least three books on your topic.
- Look for articles in magazines or newspapers.
- Ask an adult to help you look on the Internet.

Write down all the facts you find in your notebook. Remember to note where each fact came from.

The Question

The experiment you chose will have a question that looks like this:

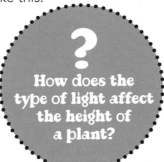

?
How does the type of light affect the height of a plant?

This question will help you come up with your *hypothesis.* The hypothesis is a guess at what you think is going to happen.

Your job is to turn that question into a statement like this:

"I think the type of light will affect the height of a plant."

Or like this:

"I think the type of light will not affect the height of a plant."

Science Fair Safety

- When in doubt, ask for help. If you're not sure that you can do something by yourself, get an adult to help you.

- Wear goggles if you're using liquids, fire, or anything that can fly through the air.

- Always wear closed-toe shoes, such as sneakers or shoes that tie. No flip-flops or sandals!

- Read the labels on household chemicals for safety warnings and directions such as "Wear gloves."

- No eating or drinking in the lab. Even if you're in the kitchen, don't eat while doing science. The food could get in your experiment and the experiment could get in you!

- Clean up before and after your experiment. Be sure your workspace is clean before you start and don't leave a mess when you're done.

Use your research to help you figure out your hypothesis. Don't worry about whether you're right or wrong. Write down your hypothesis and all the reasons you chose it in your notebook. The experiment will test your hypothesis. When you've finished your experiment, you'll have proved (you were right) or disproved (you were wrong) your hypothesis.

The Experiment

Each experiment in this book has a list of supplies (called What You Need) and step-by-step instructions. You'll need all the supplies on the What You Need list and your notebook. Usually you have to get a lot of the same thing, such as 12 plants, because you do each part of the experiment several times. These are called *trials.* The more trials you do, the more *data* you have, and the more accurate your results will be. (Data is the information you collect.) The steps in the experiment will tell you exactly what to do.

Experiment Design

There are three important parts to every experiment. Understanding what each part does will help you reach your conclusion. Before you start, read through the experiment and identify these three parts. Write what they are in your notebook.

1. The Independent Variable

The *independent variable* is what you change in the experiment. It affects what happens during each trial. The independent variable is in the first part of the question in each experiment. In our example, "How does the type of light affect the height of a plant?" the independent variable is the type of light. You'll only have one independent variable in your experiment.

2. The Dependent Variable

The *dependent variable* is what changes in the experiment when you change the independent variable. It depends on the independent variable and is always in the second part of the question. In our example, "How does the type of light affect the height of a plant?" the dependent variable is the height of the plants.

3. The Controls

You only want one thing to change in your experiment. If more things change, you won't be able to figure out exactly what happened. The experiments in this book are designed to make sure only one thing changes. The things that don't change are called the *controls.* In the plant experiment, if you use different kinds of plants, the difference in the height of the plants could be because some plants grow faster than others. To control this, use the same kind of plant. There are lots of controls in each experiment. Identify each one.

Experiment Procedure

Now you're ready to do the really fun part—the experiment! Read through all of the steps in the experiment again. Do you understand each step? Ask an adult for help if you don't. Then gather all the supplies you need for your experiment. If an experiment says ADULT SUPERVISION REQUIRED, make sure you have an adult around. Follow the steps in the experiment. Work slowly and carefully, and most of all have fun!

Recording Data

As you do the experiment, you'll collect data. Make a data table before you start taking measurements (see page 12). Leave lots of room in your table to record observations. For the plant experiment, write down the size and color of the leaves. If something unexpected happens, such as your dog knocking over one of the plants, write that down in your notebook.

The Conclusion

The Conclusion section of your experiment will help you figure out what you discovered.

Average Your Results

After you've done your experiment, you'll have a bunch of measurements from running trials over and over again. In our plant experiment, you'll have the heights of 12 different plants: six grown in sunlight and six grown in fluorescent light. That's a lot of numbers! So you'll combine the heights of all the plants that grew in the sunlight into one number, called an *average*. You'll average the plants that grew in the fluorescent light. Then you'll only have two numbers to compare! If you have a

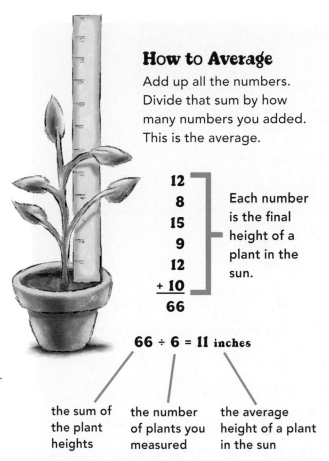

How to Average

Add up all the numbers. Divide that sum by how many numbers you added. This is the average.

$$
\begin{array}{r}
12 \\
8 \\
15 \\
9 \\
12 \\
+\ 10 \\
\hline
66
\end{array}
$$

Each number is the final height of a plant in the sun.

$66 \div 6 = 11$ inches

the sum of the plant heights

the number of plants you measured

the average height of a plant in the sun

measurement that's really different from your other measurements, you can throw it out. This is called an *outlier*. (Scientists do this all the time.)

Make a Graph to Show Your Results

When you put your data in a graph, you can really see what happened in your experiment. There are several different kinds of graphs, and the one you should use depends on the type of data you have. There are examples of each kind of graph on pages 12 and 13.

Questions

At the end of the Conclusion, there are questions for you to answer. Write down the answers in your lab notebook. Is your hypothesis supported or not? If your experiment disagrees with your hypothesis, don't worry! The judges won't count that against you at the fair. How you did your experiment is just as important as the conclusion.

Explore Further

Some experiments have an Explore Further section that gives you lots of cool ideas for other ways to do your experiment.

Take a Closer Look

In this section, you'll find information about why your experiment turned out the way it did. This section won't tell you the answer—that's what the experiment is for! It will help you explore the science behind what happened in your experiment though.

Prepare for the Fair

Congratulations! You've finished your experiment. Now it's time to share what you discovered. This section will give you some tips for writing your report and making a display.

Write Your Report

This is simple—look in your lab notebook! All the information is written down in there.

Title Page

Your title should be short and to the point. Don't make it longer than your report! Use your research question for the title if you want. Put your name, grade, the date, and your school on the title page.

Abstract

The *abstract* says what your experiment was about and what you found out.

Introduction

The introduction is where you explain what you wanted to explore. How did you choose this topic? Why is this an important subject to study?

Procedure

This is the story of how you did your experiment, not instructions for doing it again. Describe what you did, what you measured, and what materials you used. What were your dependent and independent variables? What were your controls and how did you control them? This is also a good place to put a drawing or photo of your setup. Be sure to label all the parts.

Data

Put your data or your graphs here. Label everything and write down the units of measurement (inches, minutes, etc.).

Discuss Your Data

What do your graphs and tables show? Point out any patterns or trends you want the reader (or the judges) to notice. Describe your observations here, too.

Conclusion

Explain what it all means and answer your research question. Then answer these questions: What would you do differently? Did you come up with more questions than answers? What are some ideas for further research?

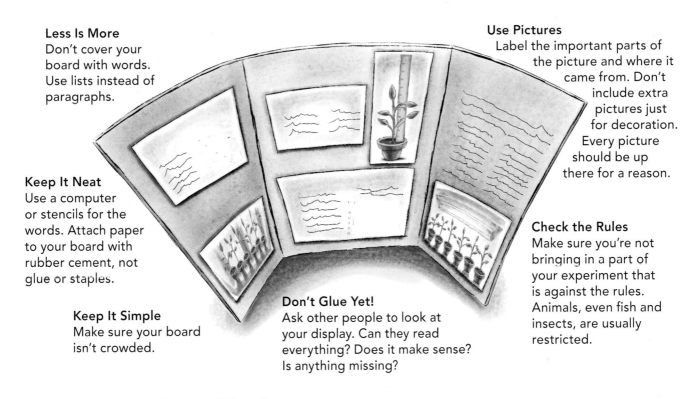

Less Is More
Don't cover your board with words. Use lists instead of paragraphs.

Keep It Neat
Use a computer or stencils for the words. Attach paper to your board with rubber cement, not glue or staples.

Keep It Simple
Make sure your board isn't crowded.

Don't Glue Yet!
Ask other people to look at your display. Can they read everything? Does it make sense? Is anything missing?

Use Pictures
Label the important parts of the picture and where it came from. Don't include extra pictures just for decoration. Every picture should be up there for a reason.

Check the Rules
Make sure you're not bringing in a part of your experiment that is against the rules. Animals, even fish and insects, are usually restricted.

Put Together Your Display

You'll need a display to take to the fair. This is usually a three-paneled, freestanding board. You can get one at office or school supply stores.

Check with your teacher for rules on the space and size for your display. You don't want to get disqualified because your display is too big!

Tips for Talking to the Judges

Explain your abstract (the short version of your experiment) to the judges. Then walk them through your hypothesis, procedure, data, and conclusions. Mention any interesting questions that came up during your experiment.

- Talk slowly and clearly.
- Don't read off your display.
- Explain what everything is and how it relates to your experiment.
- Relax and smile!

The Judges

The science fair judges will walk around the fair and talk to you about your experiment. Don't be scared! The judges are on your side. They want to see how well you've done.

Above all, be honest. Don't try to cover up the errors you made. Explain what they were and how you would do things differently if you had more time. If you don't know the answer to a question, that's okay! It's better to admit you don't know than to try to make something up. (The judges will know.) Be proud of the good work you've done.

Tables & Graphs

Tables and graphs are a good way to organize your data. There are several different ways to create tables and graphs. The kind you use depends on the type of data you have. Each experiment will tell you which kind to use and will help you make it.

Plant Height

Type of Light	Which Plant	Plant Height (day 0)	Plant Height (day 1)	Plant Height (day 2)	Plant Height (day 3)	Plant Height (day 4)	Plant Height (day 5)	Plant Height (day 6)	Plant Height (day 7)
Sunlight	Plant 1	3"	3.5"	4.5"	6.5"	8.75"	11"	11"	12"
Sunlight	Plant 2	3"	3.5"	4.5"	6.5"	8.75"	11"	11"	12"
Sunlight	Plant 3	3"	4.25"	5"	7.5"	11"	14"	14"	15"
Sunlight	Plant 4	3"	3"	3.75"	5"	6"	8"	8"	9"
Sunlight	Plant 5	3"	3.75"	4.5"	6.5"	9"	11"	11"	12"
Sunlight	Plant 6	3"	3.5"	4.25"	6"	8"	9"	9"	10"

Data Tables

Use a *data table* to write down your measurements and observations as you do the experiment. Make a data table in your lab notebook. Put the independent variable in the left column. Put the dependent variable in the columns to the right. Give the table a title. Label each row and column.

A data table isn't always the best way to show off your numbers when you're done though. A big table full of numbers is really hard to look at. If you have fewer than five numbers, you can keep your data in the table. Otherwise, use the averages of your results to make this table.

Average Plant Height

Type of Light	Day 0	Day 1	Day 2	Day 3	Day 4	Day 5	Day 6	Day 7	Total Growth
Fluorescent Light Bulb	3"	3.5"	4.5"	6.5"	8.75"	11"	12"	12"	9"
Sunlight	3"	4.25"	5"	7.5"	11"	14"	15"	15"	12"

Bar Graph

When your independent variables are names or things rather than numbers, a *bar graph* is the way to go. There are two important parts to a bar graph. The *X axis* is the line along the bottom of the page. The *Y axis* is the line that goes up the side of the page. The X axis is where the independent variable goes. The experiment will help you figure out what to put on the X axis and what to put on the Y axis. Label the axes and don't forget the units of measurement!

Line Graph

A *line graph* works a lot like a bar graph. It's good for showing patterns, or how data changed over time. When your independent variable is a number or an amount, use a line graph. The X axis is the line along the bottom of the page. The Y axis is the line that goes up the side of the page. The experiment will help you figure out what to put on the X axis and what to put on the Y axis. Be sure to label the axes and don't forget to include the units of measurement!

If you have more than one set of data, you can either make two different graphs, or you can put two lines (one for each set of data) on the same graph. If you use the same graph, make each line a different color, and label which is which.

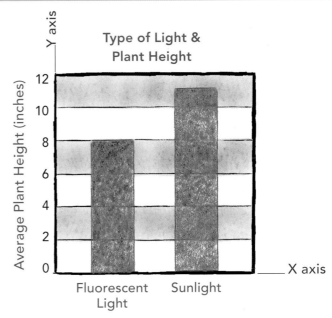

This bar graph shows how the type of light affected the height of the plant.

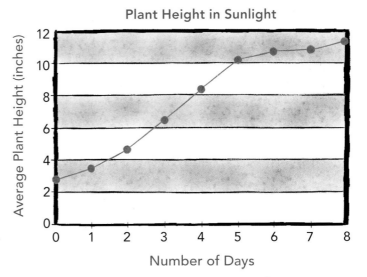

This line graph shows how the height of the plant changed over eight days.

Red Eye

Why do some people have red eyes in photographs?

? Does eye color affect red eye in a photograph?

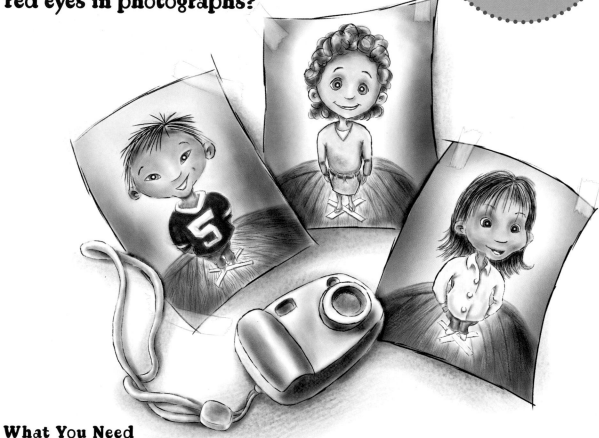

What You Need

- Masking tape
- Measuring tape
- Room with an overhead light
- Camera with flash
- Film (if the camera is not digital)
- 4 volunteers with blue eyes
- 4 volunteers with brown eyes
- 4 volunteers with hazel-green eyes
- Clock or stopwatch

Experiment

1 Using the masking tape, make two Xs on the floor about 4 feet (1.2 m) away from each other in the center of the room.

2 If your camera has a red-eye reduction feature, turn it off. Turn on the flash.

3 Turn off all of the lights in the room except the overhead light. Close the blinds on any windows.

4 Have your first volunteer stand on one of the Xs. Write down the color of his eyes.

5 Stand on the other X. Take three photos of his face. Wait at least three minutes between taking each photo.

6 Repeat steps 4 and 5 with each of your volunteers.

7 Get the film developed or download the pictures. Look carefully at each photograph. Some of your volunteers will appear to have a bright red circle where their *pupil* should be. Next to where you wrote the volunteer's eye color, write down if there's any red eye in each photograph you took.

Conclusion

Group the photographs of each eye color together. Make sure you have an equal number of photos for each eye color. Count how many photographs had red eye for each eye color. Make a bar graph to show your results. On the X axis, write the eye colors you tested. On the Y axis, put the number of photos with red eye. Which eye color had the most red-eye photos? Which eye color had the fewest red-eye photos? Why do you think that is?

Do you notice any difference in how the red eye appears in the photo? That is, are some eyes redder than others? Is the whole pupil red or is there just a ring? Is it a solid red or a fuzzy red?

EXPLORE FURTHER

Does the brightness or angle of the light affect red eye? Take photos when the room is dim and when it's bright. Place a lamp in front of the person, next to the person, and behind the person. Do any of these setups get rid of the red eye? Are people of Asian, African, or European descent more likely to have red eye even if they all have brown eyes? Do animals have red eye in photos? If you can, use the red-eye reduction feature on your camera. Does it work?

TAKE A CLOSER LOOK

Eye color is determined by the amount of *melanin* in the iris. Lighter color eyes have less melanin than darker color eyes.

When you take a flash photograph, the bright light zooms through the pupil into your eyeball before the *iris* can close. The light bounces off the *retina* in the back of your eye. The retina is full of blood vessels so the light turns red. The red eye you see in the photograph is actually the retina, not the iris and pupil that you usually see.

The red-eye reduction feature on some cameras gives two flashes instead of one. The first flash makes the iris close so the light doesn't make it to the retina.

Some animals, such as cats and some dogs, have an extra layer behind their retina to help them see better in the dark. This layer can make their eyes look pink, green, yellow, or even blue in flash photographs!

Why did the teacher's eyes cross?

She couldn't control her pupils!

15

Eggs to Dye For

Why wait for Easter?
You can dye eggs right now!

What You Need

- 12 raw eggs
- Pot (enamel or teflon coated is best)
- Measuring cup
- Water
- Measuring spoons
- Ground turmeric
- Adult helper
- Stove
- Clock or stopwatch
- Big spoon
- Paper towels
- White vinegar
- Alum*
- Permanent marker

You can find this on the baking aisle at the grocery store.

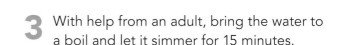

Experiment

1 Put three of the eggs in the pot. Add 1 cup (200 mL) of water at a time until the eggs are covered. Write down how much water you put in the pot. Use this amount of water every time you dye the eggs.

2 Add 2 tablespoons (30 mL) of ground turmeric to the water.

3 With help from an adult, bring the water to a boil and let it simmer for 15 minutes.

4 Have your adult helper take the eggs out of the pot and pat them dry with a paper towel. Set them aside to cool while you continue the experiment.

5 Clean out the pot and repeat steps 1 through 4 with three new eggs, but this time add 2 teaspoons (10 mL) of white vinegar and the 2 tablespoons (30 mL) of turmeric.

6 Clean out the pot and repeat steps 1 through 4 with three new eggs, using 1 teaspoon (5 mL) of alum and 2 tablespoons (30 mL) of turmeric.

7 Clean out the pot. Repeat steps 1 through 4 with three new eggs, using 1 teaspoon (5 mL) of alum, 2 teaspoons (10 mL) of white vinegar, and 2 tablespoons (30 mL) of turmeric. (Because your experiment tests which ingredient works best, the differing amounts of vinegar and alum don't count as a variable. They're just the amounts that make the experiment work best.)

8 When all the eggs are cool, use a permanent marker to label them so that you know if they were dyed with vinegar, alum, both, or neither.

9 Put the eggs in order from lightest to darkest and write down your results.

10 Scrub the eggs under running water and pat them dry with a paper towel.

11 Repeat step 9 after you've cleaned the eggs. Did the color stay on the eggs?

Conclusion

Which recipe for dyeing eggs gives the brightest colors? Did your results change at all after you scrubbed the eggs? Do you recommend adding vinegar, alum, or both when dyeing eggs?

EXPLORE FURTHER

Try different amounts of ground turmeric, alum, and vinegar to get the brightest color. What happens if you add baking soda or cream of tartar? What if you cook some eggs for five minutes and some for two hours? Does scrubbing the egg with soap and a scrubbing brush before you dye it make a difference? Experiment with using other natural materials as dye. Try beets, cranberries, raspberries, yellow or red onion skins, orange peels, carrot tops, cumin, apple peels, blueberries, red cabbage leaves, spinach, grape juice, and coffee grounds. Dye different types of fabric or paper.

TAKE A CLOSER LOOK

People have been dyeing eggs for a long time to celebrate the return of spring. Before they could buy dyes in the grocery store, they had to use what they could find in their gardens. Ancient peoples used clay, rust, and ash to dye their eggs. They also used these materials to dye clothes and pottery.

To make the colors bright and long-lasting, chemicals called *mordants* were added to the dyes. The mordants make the color stick to the egg. In this experiment, the vinegar and alum are the mordants. The turmeric dyes the eggs yellow. Which mordant works best?

Why did the chicken cross the road? Because the rooster egged her on.

Gooey Dough Ball

What do you like more, cake or pizza? They taste very different, but they have one important thing in common—gluten!

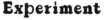
?

How does the type of flour affect how much gluten can be removed?

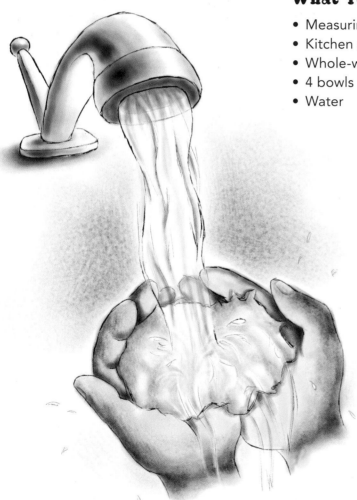

What You Need

- Measuring cup
- Kitchen scale
- Whole-wheat flour
- 4 bowls
- Water
- Clock or stopwatch
- Sink
- Cookie sheet
- Oven
- Bread flour
- All-purpose flour
- Pastry flour

Experiment

1 Weigh the measuring cup on the kitchen scale. Write down the weight.

2 Add 1 cup (200 mL) of whole-wheat flour to the measuring cup. Weigh the cup and the flour. Subtract the weight of the cup (from step 1). Write down the weight of the flour.

3 Pour the whole-wheat flour in the first bowl. Add ¾ cup (177 mL) of water. Use your hands to mix the flour and water until you get a soft, rubbery ball. Let the ball sit on the counter for 10 minutes.

4 Hold the ball in your hand over the sink and run cold water over it. Be careful to hold the ball together by cupping your hands around it. Gently squeeze the ball to remove the starch. The water dissolves the starch. That's why the water turns white.

Stop when the water runs clear and the ball is a sticky, slimy web of gluten strands. Now the ball is almost pure gluten!

5 Play with the ball. Write down how it feels, stretches, looks, bounces, and anything else you observe.

6 Place the gluten ball on a cookie sheet. Bake it in the oven at 450°F (232°C) for about 20 minutes, or until the gluten ball is dry and hardened. Write down what changed about the gluten ball.

7 Weigh the dried gluten ball. Write down how much it weighs.

8 Repeat steps 2 through 7 to test the bread flour, all-purpose flour, and pastry flour.

Conclusion

Calculate how much of the original flour ball was gluten by using this formula:

Weight of gluten ball ÷ Weight of flour ball x 100
example: 8 oz ÷ 12 oz = .67
.67 x 100 = 67%

This equation gives you the percent of the flour ball that is gluten. The rest of the ball (all the stuff you washed down the drain) is starch. Calculate the percentage of gluten in the flour ball for each type of flour. Write down the percentages in your notebook.

Make a bar graph to show your results. Put the type of flour on the **X** axis and the percent of gluten in each flour ball on the **Y** axis. Which flour had the most gluten? Which had the least?

EXPLORE FURTHER
Try measuring the gluten in other types of flour such as instant flour, gluten flour, or flour from other grains like oats or barley.

TAKE A CLOSER LOOK
Look closely at a piece of bread. Do you see tiny bubbles? These little pockets make bread fluffy. When bread is rising, the yeast in the dough makes gas. The gluten fills up with the gas, just like a balloon fills up when you blow air into it.

When the gluten balloons expand, they make the bread rise. Flours with lots of gluten will make more balloons to trap gas, and the balloons will be bigger. So the more gluten flour has in it, the more it will rise.

Think about the difference between a cake and a pizza crust. The cake is really fluffy, but the pizza crust is flat and dense. Bakers need lots of gluten for breads and cakes but very little for pizza crusts, piecrusts, and pastries. Based on your experiment, which flour would you use for cakes? Which would you use to make a pizza crust?

Do you like raisin bread?
Don't know, I never raised any.

Hear, Hear!

What if you had three, four, or even more ears? Would you have super hearing or would you just look funny?

?
How does the number of ears you are using affect how well you can tell how far away a sound is?

What You Need

- Tape
- Quiet room
- Measuring tape
- Marker
- 5 or more volunteers
- Blindfold
- Cotton balls

Experiment

1 Make an X with tape on the floor of a quiet room.

2 Use the tape to mark spots on the floor going away from the **X** in a straight line. Make a mark every 5 feet (1.5 m). Do this until you run out of room. Label how far away each mark is from the **X**.

3 Have your first volunteer stand on the **X**, facing the marks you made. Cover his eyes with the blindfold. Tell him he has to keep his head still during the entire experiment.

4 Stand on one of the marks away from the X and say the volunteer's name in a normal voice. Don't whisper or shout. Make sure you use the same voice each time you say the volunteer's name. Ask him to tell you which mark you're standing on. Record whether the guess was right but don't tell him where you're standing.

5 Repeat step 4 for all the marks at least twice. Be sure to mix it up!

6 Now have the volunteer put a cotton ball in his right ear and repeat steps 4 and 5. Remind your volunteer to keep his head still. He can't turn toward the sound to help figure out where you are.

7 Repeat step 6 with the cotton ball in your volunteer's left ear.

8 Repeat steps 3 through 7 with the rest of your volunteers.

Conclusion

Count how many times each volunteer guessed right using both ears, just his left ear, and just his right ear. Make a bar graph to show your results. Put the ears used on the X axis (both ears, left ear, right ear) and the number of correct guesses on the Y axis. If one of your volunteer's results were really different from the rest, consider throwing away their results and getting a new volunteer.

Why can't you tell a secret in a cornfield?

Because there are too many ears!

EXPLORE FURTHER

Can the volunteers tell the distance of the sound if you whisper or yell? What if you're outside where there are other noises or if the TV or radio is playing? What if the volunteer turns sideways so the different distances are just on one side of his head?

Try the experiment with grown-ups and kids. Which group is better at telling where the sound is? If you know someone with a hearing aid, see if he's any better at finding sounds than people who don't have one.

TAKE A CLOSER LOOK

Your brain uses the loudness of a sound to figure out how far away it is. Louder sounds are usually closer. Quieter sounds are usually farther away. You can try to trick your volunteers by speaking quieter when you are close and louder when you are far away. (Since this introduces another variable to your experiment, don't use this data to come to your conclusion.)

When you hear, a sound may get to one ear just a little bit earlier than it gets to the other. This small difference in time tells your brain where a sound is coming from. If the sound comes from your right side, it'll get to your right ear before it gets to your left ear.

Paint the House

? How does the color of your house affect the inside temperature?

What color is your house? Would you save energy if you painted it a different color?

What You Need

- Gray, white, and black house paint
- Paintbrush
- 3 shoeboxes, all the same size
- 4 thermometers
- Table
- Clock or stopwatch
- Heat lamp
- Ruler
- Cookie sheet
- Ice
- White plastic grocery bag

Experiment

1 For each color of paint, find the Light Reflectance Value (LRV) on the paint can. This is how much light the paint will reflect. Write down the LRV of each paint.

2 Paint the outside of each box. Paint one gray, one white, and one black. Let the paint dry completely.

3 Put a thermometer inside each box and another on the table next to the boxes.

Let them sit for 15 minutes so that they're all at room temperature. Write down the starting temperature. (The thermometers should be showing approximately the same temperature.)

4 Position the heat lamp so it shines on all the boxes and the extra thermometer. Use the ruler to make sure that all the boxes are the same distance from the lamp. Move the boxes if you need to.

5 Let the lamp shine on the boxes for 30 minutes. Then write down the temperature on all the thermometers. This is your summer temperature.

6 Turn off the lamp and let the boxes and thermometers cool down for 15 minutes.

7 Fill the cookie sheet with a layer of ice and cover it with the white plastic bag. This will imitate frozen, snow-covered ground in winter.

8 Place the boxes on top of the white plastic bag and arrange them as you did in step 4. Place the extra thermometer on top of the "snow." Turn on the heat lamp again.

9 Let the lamp shine on the boxes for 30 minutes. Then write down the temperature on all the thermometers. This is your winter temperature.

Conclusion

Make a bar graph to show how the house color affected the temperature for winter and summer. Put the house color on the **X** axis and the temperature on the **Y** axis. Make a line graph to show how the LRV affected the temperature for winter and summer. Put the LRV of each paint color on the **X** axis and the temperature on the **Y** axis. How did the temperature inside the boxes compare to the temperature outside the boxes? Does the temperature increase or decrease with the LRV number? Which colors should you use in places with hot weather? Which colors should you use in places with cold weather? What about places that have hot summers and cold winters? What color should your house be?

EXPLORE FURTHER

Coat your boxes with building materials such as adobe, stucco, wood, siding, or metal. What happens when you put different types of shingles on top of the boxes?

TAKE A CLOSER LOOK

Most of the energy your family uses goes into heating and cooling your house. In general, light colors *reflect* sunlight, bouncing it back so that the building stays cool. Dark colors *absorb* sunlight, soaking it up so the building warms up. You can lower your energy bill by changing the color of your house! Changing the color of the inside can make a difference, too. If you paint your room a cool color like blue or green, you might feel cooler than the real temperature and rooms that are red, pink, or orange can seem warmer.

What did the paint say to the house?

I've got you covered!

23

Make Dessert First

If you want to eat your gelatin dessert as soon as you can, what kind of fruit should you put in it?

What You Need

- Adult helper
- Knife
- 1 fresh peach
- 1 can of peaches
- 1 fresh pear
- 1 can of pears
- 1 fresh pineapple
- 1 can of pineapple rings
- 1 fresh mango
- Measuring cup
- Steamer or pot for boiling water
- Water
- 8 packages of sugar-free gelatin dessert mix, 3 ounces (85 g) each*
- 8 medium-sized bowls
- Clock or stopwatch

Each package should be the same flavor.

Experiment

1 With help from an adult, cut all of the fruits into bite size pieces. Keep the canned and fresh fruits separate.

2 Measure out 1 cup (200 mL) of each fruit. For each fruit you should have 1 cup (200 mL) of fresh fruit and 1 cup (200 mL) of canned fruit. For the mango, set aside 1 cup (200 mL) of fresh mango and have your adult helper boil or steam another cup of mango for about five minutes. (This is what happens to the other fruit when it's canned.)

3 Prepare the gelatin dessert mix following the directions on the box. Put in the fruit after you've dissolved all the mix. Label each of the eight bowls with the type of fruit and exactly what time you added the fruit. Place the bowls in the refrigerator.

4 Check the bowls every 10 minutes. The dessert has "set" when it's more like a solid than a liquid. Test to see if the dessert has set by gently placing your finger on the surface of the dessert. If some of the dessert sticks to your finger, it hasn't set yet. If your finger stays clean, the dessert has set. Write down how long it took the dessert to set.

5 Subtract the time you added the fruit from the time the dessert was set. This is the "set time." Do this for each bowl.

Conclusion

Make a bar graph to show your results. Put the fruit type on the **X** axis and the set time on the **Y** axis. Which fruit took the longest to set? Which fruit set the fastest? Did any of the fruits never set? What fruits would be best to use in gelatin dessert?

EXPLORE FURTHER

What else affects how long it takes gelatin dessert to set? Try putting the dessert in the fridge, freezer, or just leaving it on the counter to test the effect of temperature on set time. Do different flavors take longer to set than others? How about sugar-free versus sugar-full? Try different brands of gelatin dessert mix.

TAKE A CLOSER LOOK

All living things, including fruits, contain *enzymes*. Enzymes are chemicals that help the fruits grow and ripen. Some fruits contain an enzyme that *digests* gelatin. If you add a fruit with the gelatin-digesting enzyme, the gelatin dessert won't set. Canning or cooking the fruit destroys the enzyme. Then your gelatin is safe and your dessert will wiggle again! Which of your fruits had gelatin-eating enzymes?

What happened when the scientist put dynamite in the fridge?

It blew its cool!

The Eyes Have It

The average person eats more than 120 pounds (54.4 kg) of potatoes every year! How can we grow enough potatoes for everyone?

?
How does the amount of potato affect root growth?

What You Need

- 8 potatoes, all about the same size
- 20 paper bags
- Tape
- Marker
- Adult helper
- Knife

Experiment

1 Put four of the potatoes in four paper bags and tape the bags closed. Label each bag "Whole Potato."

2 With an adult's help, cut two of the potatoes in half so that you have four potato pieces. Put each piece in a different bag. Label the bags and tape them closed. Label each bag "Half Potato."

3 With an adult's help, cut one potato in quarters so that you have four potato

pieces. Put each piece in a different bag. Label the bags and tape them closed. Label each bag "Quarter Potato."

4 With an adult's help, cut one potato into eighths so that you have eight potato pieces. Put each piece in a different bag. Label the bags and tape them closed. Label each bag "Eighth Potato."

5 Leave the bags in a cool, dry room for two weeks.

6 Open the bags and count how many roots are on each piece of potato. Write down the size of the potato pieces and how many roots each piece has.

Why did the farmer plant his potatoes in bags?

So they wouldn't get dirt in their eyes!

Conclusion

Calculate the average number of roots for each size of potato (see page 9). Make a line graph to show your results. Put the number of roots on the X axis and the size of the potato pieces on the Y axis. Which size potato produced the most roots? Which produced the least number of roots?

Put the pieces of potato back together, so each one forms the original potato again. Then count the total number of roots for that potato. How does this compare to the number of roots on a whole potato? Make another line graph to show these results. Put the potato piece size on the Y axis and the total number of roots for a whole potato on the X axis.

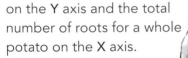

EXPLORE FURTHER

Experiment with other root vegetables, such as carrots, turnips or onions, sweet potatoes, and red potatoes.

Potatoes and other plants produce a chemical called *auxin* that helps roots grow. You can buy auxin at plant stores. Does applying auxin to the potato affect how many roots grow?

TAKE A CLOSER LOOK

Just what are potatoes anyway? They're actually the root of the potato plant. That's why they're always dirty when you buy them at the grocery store—they grow under ground. Potato plants make flowers like most other plants, but the flowers don't produce seeds to make a new plant. Instead, new potato plants come from planting a piece of potato with the beginning of a root growing. (This is called an eye.) You probably saw eyes on the potato pieces you used in the experiment. After doing this experiment, do you think a farmer should plant a whole potato for each new potato plant she wants to grow, or should she cut up a few potatoes and plant lots of little pieces?

What Stinks?

Some smells make your mouth water. Other smells make you want to run away. Do some smells reach you faster than others?

?
How does the type of smell affect how fast it travels?

What You Need

- 6 smelly objects (orange peel, coffee beans, cotton balls soaked in perfume or ammonia, spices, buttered popcorn, chopped garlic or onions, burnt toast, stinky gym socks, a dirty diaper, etc.)
- 6 containers with snap-fit lids
- Chair
- Measuring tape
- 5 or more volunteers
- Stopwatch
- Fan

Experiment

1 Put each object in a container and close the lid so the smell doesn't escape.

2 Place the chair at one end of a room in your house and the closed containers at the other end—as far away as possible. Use the measuring tape to measure how far apart they are. Write down the distance.

3 Have your first volunteer sit in the chair.

4 Tell the volunteer what smell you'll open first. Ask her to tell you as soon as she smells it.

5 Open the container and start the stopwatch. Stop the stopwatch when the volunteer tells you she smells it. Write down the time and what you had her smell.

6 Close the container and run the fan for two minutes to clear the air.

7 Repeat steps 4 through 6 for each of the smelly objects.

8 Repeat steps 3 through 7 for each of your volunteers.

Conclusion

Average the time it took each of the smells to reach your volunteers (see page 9). If one person's results are way off, throw the results out and test a new volunteer. That one probably has a cold!

To find out how fast each smell traveled, divide the distance between the chair and containers (from step 2) by the average time it took for each smell to get to the volunteers. For example, if the chair was 24 feet (7.3 m) from the coffee beans and it took your volunteers an average of 6 seconds to smell it, the speed is

24 feet (7.3 m) ÷ 6 seconds =
4 feet (1.2 m) per second.

Make a bar graph to show your results. Put the types of smell on the **X** axis and the speeds on the **Y** axis. Which smells traveled the quickest? Which smells traveled the slowest? Does the speed depend on whether the smells are sweet or super stinky? What else did you observe about the smells?

EXPLORE FURTHER

Do your volunteers take longer to detect the smell if you don't tell them what it is? Do the experiment with kids and grown-ups. Does age affect how quickly you can detect a smell? Do smells travel faster outdoors or indoors? What if the air is hot or cold?

TAKE A CLOSER LOOK

When you smell something, a tiny particle of it is actually going up your nose! Tiny smell particles float off things and travel through the air. They move around randomly until they reach your nose. There are more particles closer to the object than there are farther away. This means you'll smell an object more quickly if you're close to it. Other things affect how fast a smell travels: the size of the smell particle, how fast the air is moving, and the temperature. Since you're doing all the experiments in the same room, the air speed and the temperature stay the same throughout the experiment.

Once the smell particles get to your nose, they get soaked up by the *mucus* (snot!) in your nose. *Epithelial olfactory receptor* cells (smell cells) in your nose detect the smell particles in your snot and tell your brain what the smell is. Some smells bypass the snot and go straight into the smell cells.

What did one eye say to the other?

Between you and me... something smells!

Taste Test

?

How does the place on your tongue affect what you taste?

Sometimes, even scientists have to admit that they're wrong. Here's an experiment that proves something scientists thought was true for a long time isn't.

What You Need

- Tablespoon
- Sugar
- 2 glasses
- Water
- Salt
- 5 or more volunteers*
- Toothpicks
- Glass of water

Make sure all of your volunteers are healthy! If anybody has a runny nose or sore throat, they may not be able to taste very well.

Experiment

1 Stir 3 tablespoons (44.4 mL) of sugar into a glass of water. Stir 3 tablespoons (44.4 mL) of salt into another glass of water.

2 In your lab notebook, draw a large tongue shape for each volunteer. You'll write down your data on this picture.

3 Tell your first volunteer that you're going to touch parts of her tongue with a taste and she should tell you what she tastes.

4 Dip a toothpick into the salt water and lightly touch the tip of the tongue. Write down what she says she tastes and what you tested on the tip of the tongue you drew in step 2. It's all right if she tells you she doesn't taste anything (but be sure to write it down!). Give the volunteer a drink of water.

5 Repeat step 4, touching a different spot with the salty or sugary water. Test both on the tip, sides, middle, and back of the tongue. Use a different toothpick for each flavor of water, and use clean toothpicks for each volunteer. Be very careful testing the back part of the tongue since some people may gag. Let the volunteer drink some water between each test.

Conclusion

Compare the final tongue pictures for all of your volunteers. Are there any parts of the tongue where the sugar and salt tasted the same? Are there any parts of the tongue that only tasted the sugar or the salt?

EXPLORE FURTHER

How well does the tongue sense temperature? Try using hot, warm, room temperature, cold, and icy water to see if your volunteers' tongues can tell how cold or hot the water is. You can also test foods that taste "hot" or "cold," such as chilies or peppermint gum.

TAKE A CLOSER LOOK

For a long time scientists thought that you only tasted flavors on specific parts of your tongue. For instance, they thought you could taste sweet only on the tip of your tongue and bitter only on the back. What did your experiment show?

The whole tongue is covered with little *receptors* called taste buds. They can sense up to seven different flavors: salty, sweet, bitter, sour, savory, pungent, and astringent. (Meats and cheeses are savory, hot chilies are pungent, and unripe fruit is astringent.) Our bodies use each of these tastes to make sure we eat the right food. Savory foods are protein, which our bodies use for energy. Salty foods help us keep water in our bodies. Sweet foods are full of fat and calories that our bodies can store to use later. Sour tastes keep us from eating too much acidic food that will upset the stomach. Bitter-tasting food is often poisonous, which is why it tastes bad.

Why did the lion spit out the clown?

Because he tasted funny!

The Cereal Game

Go ahead—play with your food!

? How does the distance between two pieces of O-shaped cereal affect how they move?

What You Need

- Large, round bowl
- Water
- Stopwatch
- O-shaped cereal
- Toothpicks
- Ruler
- Helper

Experiment

1 Fill the bowl halfway with water. Set it on the counter and let it sit for 15 minutes. You want to make sure that the water is still so that it doesn't make your cereal pieces move.

2 Gently place two pieces of cereal on the water. Take two toothpicks and hold one in the center of each piece of cereal. You'll use the toothpicks to move the cereal into place.

3 Use a ruler to position the pieces of cereal in the middle of the bowl, 2 inches (5.1 cm) apart. (You may need a friend to help you with this part.)

4 Hold the cereal in place for 10 seconds so the water stops moving. Then carefully lift the toothpicks straight up.

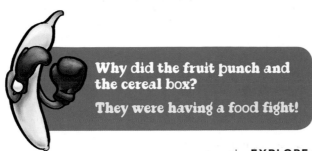

Why did the fruit punch and the cereal box?

They were having a food fight!

5 Watch the cereal pieces closely for a minute. Do they move toward each other or away? Do they stay in the same place? Write down what you see.

6 Repeat steps 1 through 5 at least four more times. Use fresh pieces of cereal each time.

7 Repeat steps 1 through 6, testing what happens when the cereal pieces are 1½ inches (3.8 cm) apart, 1 inch (2.5 cm) apart, and ½ inch (1.3 cm) apart.

Conclusion

Count how many times the cereal pieces collided for each of the distances. (If the cereal pieces don't collide, count that as 0.) Make a line graph to show your results. Put the distance between the cereal pieces on the **X** axis and the number of times they collided on the **Y** axis. How close do the cereal pieces need to be in order to collide?

EXPLORE FURTHER

Try using other liquids like soapy water, milk, corn syrup, and vegetable oil. Do other cereal shapes act the same way?

TAKE A CLOSER LOOK

Fill a clear drinking glass with water. Look carefully at the surface of the water from the side. Do you see how the water curves up the sides of the glass? This is called a *meniscus*. A meniscus is formed because the water sticks to the sides of the glass and to itself. When you float an O-shaped piece of cereal on top of water (or milk), the water curves wherever it touches the cereal, just as it curves at the sides of the glass. The piece of cereal makes a little dent (a meniscus) on the top of the water. When two pieces of cereal get close enough for the menisci to touch, they slide together. Scientists have named this "The Cheerio Effect."

Water You Drinking?

Can you drink hard water? Hard water is water that has lots of minerals in it.

?

How does location affect water hardness?

What You Need

- Water from many different places
- Measuring cup
- Clear 20-ounce soda bottles (one for each place you will collect water from)
- Permanent marker
- Dishwashing soap*
- Helper
- Stopwatch
- Ruler

Don't use "Ultra" dishwashing soap. It will make too many bubbles.

Experiment

1 Find at least four places to measure the water hardness. These places should all be very different. For example: your house, your best friend's house, your school, and the water fountain at the playground. The farther away these places are, the better.

2 Collect the water from each place. Use the measuring cup to pour exactly 1 cup (236.6 mL) of water into each soda bottle. Using the permanent marker, label each of the bottles with the place name.

3 Place two drops of dishwashing soap into the first bottle. Screw the top on very tightly. Shake the bottle as hard as you can for one minute. Have your helper time you with the stopwatch.

4 As soon as you're done shaking it, use the ruler to measure the total height of the bubbles in the bottle. In your lab notebook, write down where the water came from and the height of the bubbles. If the water is very soft, the whole bottle may be filled with bubbles. If the water is very hard, you may not have any bubbles at all. Most places will be somewhere in between.

5 Repeat steps 3 and 4 with each bottle.

Conclusion

Make a bar graph to show your results. Put where the water came from on the **X** axis and the total bubble height on the **Y** axis. Hard water will make less bubbles and soft water will make lots of bubbles. Which place had the hardest water? Which place had the softest water? Why do you think that is?

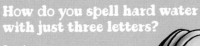

How do you spell hard water with just three letters?

Ice!

EXPLORE FURTHER

What changes if you boil the water for different times, or add lime and other water softeners from the hardware store to it before adding the dishwashing soap? Try using different types of soaps like shampoos or liquid hand soap to make the bubbles.

TAKE A CLOSER LOOK

About 85% of houses have hard water! Does yours? What other places had hard water? Hard water doesn't actually feel hard. It's called hard water because it has *minerals*, such as calcium and magnesium, in it. These minerals can make your water taste funny. Sometimes hard water eats away the metal in your pots and pans, and it can make it difficult to get a good soapy lather with your shampoo. But hard water isn't bad for you. Our bodies need certain minerals to stay healthy. Drinking hard water is one way to help your body get the calcium and magnesium it needs. A recent study suggests that drinking hard water lowers your risk of heart disease.

How do minerals end up in water? When water flows over rocks in the ground (like when it's in a river or under the ground), the minerals in the rocks *dissolve* and the water carries them around. Water without lots of minerals is called soft water. Some places use chemicals to remove the minerals. If you live near an ocean, you probably have very soft water. When the salt is removed from ocean water, the minerals are also removed.

All Cracked Up

Want an excuse to break some eggs? Do it for science!

What You Need

- Bubble wrap
- 12 raw eggs (or more if needed)
- 4 or more shoeboxes, all the same size
- Packing tape
- Adult helper
- Second story window
- Styrofoam peanuts
- Starch peanuts
- Air bags or zip-top bags

Experiment

1 Use the bubble wrap to carefully pack one of the raw eggs. Then pack it in a shoebox.

2 Tape the box closed. Go easy on the tape! You'll need to open it again to check on the egg. Plus, you'll want to reuse the box.

3 With your adult helper, hold the box out of a second-story window. Make sure there's nothing below you and that each box will land on one kind of surface (like grass or concrete, but not both). Drop the box.

4 Open the box and look at the egg. Write down what the packing material was and if the egg is whole, cracked, or broken.

5 Repeat steps 1 through 4 three more times. Use a new egg each time, even if the old one didn't break.

6 Repeat steps 1 through 5 using the styrofoam peanuts, starch peanuts, and air bags (or zip-top bags filled with air) as packing material.

Conclusion

Make a bar graph showing the results for each packing material. Put the type of damage (none, cracked, and broken) on the **X** axis. Put the number of eggs on the **Y** axis. Compare all four graphs. Which packing material protected the eggs best? Take a field trip to an office supply store and check out the costs of the different packing materials. Which is the cheapest? Based on cost and the results of your experiment, which would you recommend for packing breakable items?

Why did Humpty Dumpty have a great fall?

To make up for a bad summer!

EXPLORE FURTHER

How does the amount of packing material used affect the survival of the dropped eggs? Compare the results if you pack the eggs tightly or loosely. What if you dropped the eggs from different heights or onto different surfaces such as grass or concrete? You may even want to try mailing your packed eggs to a friend and see if they survive. Send them "special eggspress!"

TAKE A CLOSER LOOK

The *force* of the box stopping when it hits the ground is what breaks the egg. The amount of force the box needs to stop depends on three things: how fast the box is moving, how heavy it is, and how long it takes to stop. You can't change how fast the box is moving—*gravity* pulls everything at the same speed. The packing materials you used are so light they don't change the weight

of the box enough to make a difference in this experiment. What you can change is the amount of time it takes to stop the egg inside the box.

If you bang your head on the wall, it hurts. This is because the wall is hard and it stops your head very quickly. But, if you bang your head on a pillow, it doesn't hurt. The pillow is squishy and slows down your head gradually before it stops. Your head takes a longer time to stop. This experiment works the same way. After you drop the box out of the window, it falls faster and faster until the ground stops it. When you put different packing materials in the box, they act like a pillow. The packing materials give the egg more time to slow down between when the box hits the ground and when the egg hits the ground. Aren't you glad this experiment used eggs instead of your head?

All Fogged Up

How can you keep the mirror from fogging up after you shower?

?

How does rubbing soap on a mirror affect how it fogs up in a steamy bathroom?

What You Need

- Mirror (in the bathroom with the shower)
- Glass cleaner
- Masking tape
- Marker
- Adult helper
- Potato
- Paper towels
- Knife
- Bar of soap
- Shaving cream
- Liquid hand soap
- Dishwashing soap
- Shower

Experiment

1 Clean and dry the mirror with the glass cleaner.

2 Use the masking tape to divide your mirror into 6-inch (15.2 cm) squares (or bigger). You'll need six squares. (If you have a small mirror, test half of the materials. Then clean the mirror and test the other half.)

3 On the tape, label the squares with the name of each item you'll be testing. Leave one square blank. You'll compare what happens in the other squares to this one.

4 Have an adult cut the potato in half. Rub the wet part of it inside the square labeled "Potato." Use a dry paper towel to rub the mirror until it's shiny again.

5 In the square labeled "Bar of Soap," rub a dry bar of soap on the mirror. Rub the mirror with a dry paper towel until it's shiny again.

6 In the square labeled "Shaving Cream," squirt a small amount of shaving cream onto the mirror. Rub it all over the square with a dry paper towel. With another clean, dry paper towel, wipe off the extra shaving cream. Rub the mirror until it's shiny again.

Did you take a bath this morning?

No. Is there one missing?

7 Repeat step 6 to put the liquid hand soap and dishwashing soap in their squares.

8 Now it's time to get clean! Take a long hot shower. Make sure the blank square gets really steamy.

9 Write down which squares got steamy and which stayed steam-free. Leave the stuff on the mirror for the next week. Every time someone takes a shower, write down which squares stayed steam-free. Leave your notebook in the bathroom so everyone can help you record your data!

Conclusion

Which squares were steam-free after the first shower? How many showers did it take for the steam fighting power of the shaving cream, soaps, and potato to wear off? Which one lasted the longest? Make a bar graph to show your results. Put the substance on the X axis and the number of showers the mirror stayed steam-free on the Y axis. Which one would you use to keep your mirror steam-free?

EXPLORE FURTHER

Try other brands and types of soap. Which soaps keep your mirror steam-free the longest?

TAKE A CLOSER LOOK

When you take a hot shower or bath, clouds of steam form in the air. The water is so hot that it changes from water (a liquid) to steam (a gas). This is called *evaporation*. When the steam hits your cold mirror, it turns back into water and sticks to the mirror. This is called *condensation*. If you look really closely at the steamed-up mirror, you'll see teeny tiny drops of water. These tiny drops make it hard to see yourself in the mirror.

One way to keep your mirror from steaming up is to put something on the mirror that keeps the water from beading up when it condenses. Certain chemicals, like glycerin, mix with water really well. This causes the water to spread out over the mirror evenly, so you can still see yourself. Other chemicals, like oil, don't mix at all with water. This causes the water to bead up on the mirror, so you can't see yourself.

The Great Pumpkin

The best parts of Halloween (besides the candy!) are jack-o-lanterns—until they collapse into a mushy mess. Can you make your jack-o-lantern last longer?

? How does petroleum jelly affect the life of a jack-o-lantern?

What You Need

- Adult helper
- 6 pumpkins, all about the same size
- Large spoon
- Carving knife
- Measuring tape
- Petroleum jelly

Experiment

1 Get an adult to help you clean out the seeds in each pumpkin with the spoon and carve the scariest jack-o-lantern faces you can.

2 Use the measuring tape to carefully measure the height and circumference (how far around it is at its widest part) of each pumpkin.

3 Gently coat three of the pumpkins with a thin layer of petroleum jelly, inside and out. The other three pumpkins will be left plain.

4 Put all the pumpkins outdoors, somewhere safe from the rain, hungry pets, and kids who might accidentally hurt your science fair experiment.

5 Measure the height and circumference of each pumpkin every day until the jack-o-lantern faces cave in. (They might be scarier this way!)

Conclusion

For each day, calculate the average heights and circumferences for the coated pumpkins and for the plain pumpkins (see page 9). Make a line graph to show how the heights of the pumpkins changed. Make one line on the graph for the coated pumpkins and one line for the plain pumpkins. Put the day on the **X** axis and the averaged heights on the **Y** axis. Make another line graph to show how the circumference of the pumpkins changed. Put the day on the **X** axis and the average **circumference** on the **Y** axis. Make one line on the graph for the coated pumpkins and one line for the plain pumpkins.

Did the petroleum jelly affect how long the jack-o-lantern lasted? Which jack-o-lanterns, the coated or plain pumpkins, lasted the longest? Next Halloween, will you coat your jack-o-lantern with petroleum jelly?

EXPLORE FURTHER

What other coatings can you use to help your jack-o-lantern last longer? Try hair spray, acrylic craft spray, spray paint, or glue.

TAKE A CLOSER LOOK

Pumpkins have to have just the right amount of water in them. If the shell dries out, the pumpkin can collapse or cave in, just like a grape will shrivel up and turn into a raisin if it dries out. If the pumpkin gets too wet, mold can start growing on it. The mold will turn the pumpkin into a slimy, smelly mess. How do you keep just the right amount of water in your pumpkin shell?

Professional pumpkin carvers soak their jack-o-lanterns overnight in cold water and then spray them with bleach water to keep them wet and mold-free. They also store their jack-o-lanterns in the refrigerator wrapped in plastic wrap. The plastic wrap keeps the water in the shell. How long do you think a jack-o-lantern will last this way? Try it!

Did you know that the first jack-o-lanterns were actually made out of turnips? But then someone figured out it's a lot easier to carve a pumpkin than a turnip!

How do you mend a broken jack-o-lantern?

With a pumpkin patch!

Ooze

**Is ooze a liquid or a solid?
Neither—it's a colloid!**

?

**How does the type
of starch affect
the Ooze Factor of
a colloid?**

What You Need

- Tablespoon
- Cornstarch
- 4 small paper cups
- Eyedropper
- Water
- Stir sticks
- Wax paper
- Cookie sheet
- Clock or stopwatch
- Pen
- Graph paper
- Rice starch
- Potato starch
- Tapioca starch

Experiment

1 Put 4 tablespoons (60 mL) of cornstarch in a cup.

2 Use the eyedropper to add one water drop at a time to the cup. Mix the water and starch with a stir stick after you add each drop.

3 Stop adding water when the solid lumps of cornstarch start to flow together as you stir. If you stir fast, the stick seems to get stuck in cornstarch cement. If you stir slowly, the stick moves smoothly through the liquid. The substance you've made is neither a liquid nor a solid. It's called a *colloid.*

4 Put a piece of wax paper on the cookie sheet. Pour 1 tablespoon (15 mL) of the cornstarch colloid in the center of the wax paper. Let it sit for two minutes. Don't move the cookie sheet—the colloid will spread out without any help from you!

5 After two minutes, use a pen to carefully trace around the edges of the blob. Write down what kind of starch you used on the wax paper. Scrape off the colloid.

6 Put the wax paper on top of a piece of graph paper. Count how many squares the cornstarch colloid covered. (These are the squares that are inside the outline you drew in step 5.) Count all the parts of squares, too. The total number of squares the colloid covered is its Ooze Factor. This is a measure of how much the colloid blob spreads out. Write down the Ooze Factor for the cornstarch colloid.

7 Repeat steps 4 through 6 with the cornstarch colloid two more times. Use a fresh tablespoon of colloid each time. Write down the Ooze Factor for each trial.

8 Play with the cornstarch colloid. Poke at it and squish it with your fingers. Rub it between your hands and roll it on the countertop. Write down your observations.

9 Repeat steps 1 through 8 with the rice starch, potato starch, and tapioca starch.

Conclusion

Average the Ooze Factor for each type of starch colloid (see page 9). Make a bar graph to show your results. Write the type of starch on the X axis and the average Ooze Factor on the Y axis. Which starch colloid had the highest Ooze Factor? Which one had the lowest Ooze Factor? What other observations did you make about the colloids?

SIMPLIFY IT

Instead of using graph paper to measure the Ooze Factor, just trace each blob on wax paper. Then lay the wax papers on top of each other and order them from largest to smallest. (For this version, just test 1 tablespoon [15 mL] of each type of cornstarch colloid.)

TAKE A CLOSER LOOK

Colloids are all around us! Foams, gels, glue, and clay are all colloids. Some of your favorite foods are colloids, such as marshmallows, pudding, yogurt, butter, and jelly. If you pour a colloid out of a glass, it flows like a thick liquid. But if you hit the colloid quickly, it feels like a solid. Why does a colloid act like a liquid and a solid?

The starch colloids get their crazy properties from how the starch mixes with the water. The dry starch is very light and powdery. The tiny starch bits are so light, they just float in the water. They don't *dissolve* or sink to the bottom. When a lot of starch bits float in the water, they stick together. A fast, hard punch to the colloid will bounce back because you've hit a wall of starch bits. But if you lay your finger gently on top of the colloid, the starch bits will ooze out of the way and your finger will sink in.

Scientists call the Ooze Factor that you measured *viscosity*. Viscosity is just a measure of how something flows.

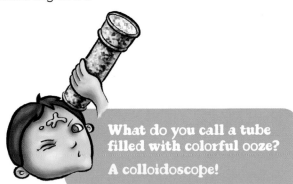

What do you call a tube filled with colorful ooze?

A colloidoscope!

43

Salt Crystals

Salt doesn't just make your food taste better. You can also use it to grow fabulous crystals!

What You Need

- Marker
- Masking tape
- 6 tall glasses
- Scissors
- String
- 6 pencils
- 6 paper clips
- Adult helper
- Boiling water
- Table salt
- Spoon
- Sea salt
- Salt substitute
- Road salt for melting ice
- Epsom salt
- Gypsum
- Clock
- Ruler

Experiment

1 Use the marker and masking tape to label each of the glasses with the salts you'll be using to grow crystals.

2 Cut six pieces of string. Each piece of string should be about 6 inches (15.2 cm) longer than the height of your glasses. Tie one end of each string to the middle of a pencil and the other end to a paper clip.

3 Have an adult pour boiling water into the glass labeled table salt so it is about ¾ full. Quickly start pouring table salt into the boiling water while you stir with the spoon. Keep adding table salt until it won't dissolve any more. You'll see pieces of salt in the bottom of the glass when this happens.

4 Repeat step 3, mixing the other salts into each glass.

5 Put the paper clip you tied to the end of the string in step 2 in the water. Roll the extra string around the pencil. Make sure the paper clip doesn't quite touch the bottom of the glass. Rest the pencil on the top of the glass. Do this for each glass.

6 Write down what time it is. This is when you started your crystals. You're going to check on them at this time every day for at least a week.

7 After 24 hours, take out the string and measure the length of your crystals with the ruler. Write down how long each crystal is. Write down anything else you notice about the size, shape, and color of the crystals. Put the paper clips and string back in the glasses when you're done.

8 Repeat step 7 every 24 hours for a week, or until the crystals stop getting longer.

Conclusion

Make a line graph for each type of salt. Put the time on the X axis and the crystal size on the Y axis. Did all of the salts make crystals? Which salt crystals grew the fastest? Which are the longest? What did you notice about the length and shape of the crystals? Why do you think they were different?

EXPLORE FURTHER

What happens if you use other chemicals, such as hydrated sodium borate (also known as borax, a cleaner you can find at the grocery store), sodium carbonate (also called washing soda), or sugar? Tie other items at the bottom of your string instead of a paper clip. Does that change the shape or length of your crystals?

TAKE A CLOSER LOOK

The first step in making crystals is to make a *supersaturated solution*. A solution is a mixture of two things. In this experiment, it's salt and water. Saturated means the water can't hold any more salt. Boiling the water helps it hold even more salt. (That's where the super comes from!)

Crystals form when the water cools and *evaporates* (changes from a liquid to a gas). Less salt can stay in the water. The salt has to go somewhere, so it sticks to the paper clip and string. The longer you wait, the more salt sticks to the paper clip, and the longer the crystals are.

Find a magnifying glass and look very closely at the salt (before it's been put in the water!). Do you see how each type of salt is already a crystal? When the tiny crystals are dissolved in water and then clump together, they make bigger crystals. What shape are the bigger crystals? Do they look like the smaller crystals?

What did the salt say to the pepper?

What's shaking?

Dominos

Do you like to topple dominos?
If so, this experiment is for you!

?

How does the pattern you use to set up dominos affect how fast they fall down?

What You Need

- 50 (or more) dominos, all the same size and weight
- Ruler
- Lots of space
- Stopwatch

Experiment

1 Stand up all of the dominos on their short ends in a straight line. Use your ruler to space the dominos ½ inch (1.3 cm) apart.

2 Start your stopwatch and tip over the first domino. Watch as it knocks down all the rest. Stop the stopwatch when the last domino falls. Write down how long it took the dominos to fall down when they were in a straight line.

3 Repeat steps 1 and 2 four more times.

4 Arrange the dominos in a circle. Make sure the dominos are ½ inch (1.3 cm) apart. Repeat steps 2 and 3.

5 Arrange the dominos in as many different shapes as you like. Try triangles, squares, circles, and wavy lines. When going around a corner or a curve, make sure that the parts of the dominos closest together are ½ inch (1.3 cm) apart.

Conclusion

Average the time it took each domino pattern to fall (see page 9). Make a line graph to show your results. Put the domino pattern (line, circle, etc.) on the **X** axis and the average fall time on the **Y** axis. Does the pattern change the time it takes the dominos to fall?

Why did the domino go to the doctor?

He was covered with spots!

EXPLORE FURTHER

What other patterns can you put the dominos in? What happens with a spiral? How does the distance between the dominos affect how fast they fall down? What is the longest distance apart you can place the dominos so they still fall down? What happens if you lay the dominos on their long sides instead of their short sides?

TAKE A CLOSER LOOK

Have you ever heard of The Domino Effect? The Domino Effect is the result of a small change (knocking over one domino) that causes more small changes (knocking over another domino, that knocks over another domino…) and ends with a big change (all the dominos have fallen down!). How fast the dominos fall down depends on how long it takes one domino to hit the next one.

Dominos were first invented in China as part of a game that involves laying the tiles flat on a table. Domino games are still played all over the world and many people also enjoy setting them up in patterns to be knocked down. In fact, in 2005, a world record was set in the Netherlands where more than four million domino tiles (also called bones) were knocked down. It took 88 people to set them all up, and they covered about 10,000 square yards (8,361 square meters). That's about the size of five football fields!

Exploding Soda

?
How does the type of soda affect the size of the explosion you get when you add mints?

Sometimes science is messy— really messy!

This experiment is very messy and must be performed outdoors.

What You Need

- A large outdoor location
- Paper
- 6 boxes of Mentos mints*
- Tape
- Index card
- 12 2-liter bottles of soda:
  - 2 types of regular soda, 3 bottles each
  - Diet versions of both regular sodas, 3 bottles each
- Measuring cup

You can try any kind of mint for this experiment, but Mentos mints work best!

Experiment

1 First, you're going to make a tube to drop the mints into the soda bottle. Roll the piece of paper into a tube about 1 inch (2.5 cm) wide. Slide a mint inside of it. If it slides in easily, tape the tube so it holds its shape. If the mint gets stuck, adjust the width of the tube until it slides in easily.

2 Put 12 mints in the tube. Hold the index card under the tube so the mints don't fall out.

3 Carefully open the first bottle of soda. Place the index card and tube of mints on top of the bottle opening.

4 Quickly slide out the index card so the mints drop in the soda bottle. If you don't want to end up covered in soda, run! Write down any observations you make about the explosion.

5 After the soda explosion is over, carefully pour the soda left in the bottle into a measuring cup. Write down how much soda was left in the bottle.

6 A 2-liter bottle holds about 8.45 cups of liquid. Subtract the amount left in the bottle from 8.45 cups. This is the amount of soda that sprayed out of the bottle.

7 Repeat steps 2 through 6 for each bottle of soda.

Conclusion

Average the amount of soda that sprayed out of the bottles of the regular soda (see page 9). Then average the amount of soda that sprayed out of the diet soda bottles. Make a bar graph to show your results. Put the type of soda on the **X** axis and the amount of soda that sprayed out on the **Y** axis. Which kind of soda gave the best explosion, diet or regular?

EXPLORE FURTHER

Can you figure out a way to measure how high the soda shoots out of the bottle? How does the number of mints affect the size of the explosion? How about the temperature of the mints? What happens if you freeze the mints or warm them briefly in the oven? Compare the explosions from different flavors of mints. What kind of explosion will you get using rock salt, table salt, or wintergreen lifesavers?

TAKE A CLOSER LOOK

When you open a bottle of soda, you can hear the fizz and see bubbles. The bubbles are caused by carbon dioxide gas *dissolved* in the soda. The soda slowly releases the gas, and the bubbles float to the surface. If you let your soda sit in a glass for a long time, all the gas is released and your soda is flat. When you shake up a bottle of soda, the gas is released faster. That's why there's more fizz and bubbles. Adding mints makes the bubbles come out of the soda even faster, because the soda releases the gas more quickly. When the gas comes out quickly, it takes the soda with it. The faster the gas comes out, the bigger the explosion.

Why is there a difference in the size of the explosion regular and diet soda makes? Regular soda is sweetened with sticky corn syrup. Diet soda is made with different kinds of artificial sweeteners. Which type of sweetener holds onto the gas better?

How do scientists freshen their breath?

With experi-mints!

It's in the Bag

How much stuff can you put into a garbage bag before you have to take it out to the trash can?

What You Need

- Large box
- Adult helper
- 4 or more brands of garbage bags with handles, all the same size
- Sand
- Scale

Experiment

1 Place the box on the floor. Have your adult helper hold the first garbage bag by the handles above the box.

2 Slowly pour sand into the bag. The bag will start to stretch and tear. Go slowly. You want to add just enough sand to make it break and no more.

3 When the bag breaks, remove all the pieces of broken bag from the box of sand. Be careful to leave all of the sand in the box. Look closely at the broken bag. Write down what you see and keep the pieces to compare to the other bags.

4 Weigh the box of sand on the scale. Write down the weight and the type of bag in your notebook. Pour out the sand.

5 Repeat steps 1 through 4 with five more of the same brand of garbage bag.

6 Repeat steps 1 through 5, testing each brand of garbage bag.

Conclusion

Average the weight of the sand it took to break each brand of garbage bag (see page 9). Since all of the bags are the same size, the weight of the sand that broke the bag can be used to measure the bag's strength. Make a bar graph to show your results. Put the brand of bag on the X axis and the strength (the amount of sand it took to break the bag) on the Y axis. How do the bags compare? What observations did you make about the bags that might explain your results? Which brand of bag would you buy?

EXPLORE FURTHER

Try using other heavy objects to break the bag like bricks or hand weights. Do you get the same results as with sand?

How stretchy are the bags? Use a ruler and measure how far you can stretch the bags before they break. How does this compare to how much sand the bags can hold?

TAKE A CLOSER LOOK

All garbage bags claim to be strong, but what exactly does that mean? There are many types of strength. Think about the difference between a garbage bag and a CD case. If you push or pull on a garbage bag, it will rip. But if you push or pull on a CD case, what happens? Nothing! The scientific way to say this is that the CD case has more tensile strength than the garbage bag. If you bend a garbage bag, nothing happens. But if you bend a CD case, it breaks. This means the garbage bag has more flexural strength than the CD case. If you twist a garbage bag, nothing happens. But if you twist a CD case, it breaks. This means the garbage bag has more torsional strength than the CD case.

Both the garbage bag and the CD case are strong. They're just strong in different ways. Why is it important for a garbage bag to be able to twist and bend? Why is it important for a CD case to stand up to pushing and pulling?

What has four wheels and flies? A garbage truck!

Candy Melt

Wait until you've finished this experiment before you eat the leftover candy!

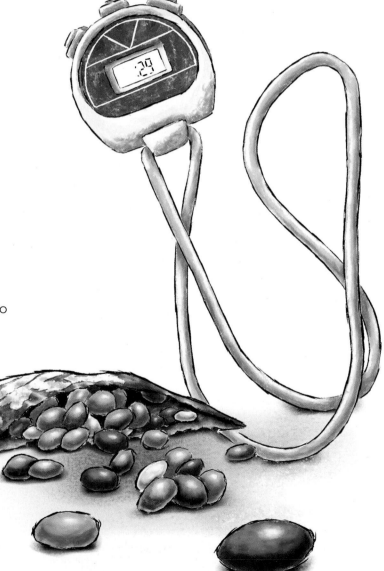

? How does candy color affect how long it takes to dissolve?

What You Need

- Pitcher
- Water
- Adult helper
- Knife
- Bag of different-colored candy-coated chocolates
- Camera (optional)
- 6 clear cups, all the same size
- Ruler
- Stopwatch

Experiment

1 Fill a pitcher with water and let it sit on a counter overnight. This will give you a good supply of room temperature water to use for all your trials.

2 Have your adult helper use a sharp knife to cut a candy in half. Do this for each color. Draw a picture or take a photo of each piece of candy.

3 Feel the shell of each color. Do the different colors feel the same or different? Write down how each one feels.

4 Pour 1½ inches (3.8 cm) of water into each cup. Separate six pieces of each color of candy.

5 Get your stopwatch ready. Quickly place one candy in the middle of each cup. All the candies should be the same color. Start your stopwatch as soon as the candies are in the water.

6 Write down how long it takes each of the candy shells to completely melt or *dissolve* in the water. Watch the candies as the shells dissolve. Write down what you see or take photos.

7 Once all of the candy shells have dissolved, empty the cups and wash them out.

8 Repeat steps 4 through 7 for each of the candy-shell colors.

9 Eat the rest of the candy.

Conclusion

Calculate the average time it took each color of candy shell to dissolve (see page 9). Make a bar graph to show your results. Put the candy-shell color on the **X** axis and the time it takes to dissolve on the **Y** axis. Which color dissolved the slowest? Which dissolved the fastest? What did you observe while the colors dissolved? What did you observe when the candies were cut in half?

Why did the cookie go to the doctor?

Because it was feeling crummy.

EXPLORE FURTHER

Try other types of coated candies. Does the size of the cup or the water temperature affect how fast the candy shells dissolve? If you have a candy in your mouth and a candy in your hand, which one melts faster? Breath fresheners now come in strips that dissolve on your tongue. Test how long it takes the strips to dissolve and compare them to other types of breath fresheners.

TAKE A CLOSER LOOK

The water dissolved the candy shells. There are lots of reasons some candy shells dissolve faster than others. The biggest factor in how quickly the shells dissolve is how thick the shells are. Thicker candy shells have more candy, so it'll take longer for them to melt into the water. Smooth shells take longer to dissolve than rough shells because rough shells have more places for the water to grab onto. Different colors of candy shells are made of different sized particles. Smaller particles dissolve faster than larger particles. Try dissolving regular sugar and powdered sugar in water. The powdered sugar will dissolve a lot faster! Why do you think some of your candies dissolved faster than others?

The candy shell on the outside of a chocolate is a lot like the coatings chemists put on medicine. Chemists are always looking for the perfect coatings for pills. Sometimes they want a medicine to dissolve quickly when it's in your mouth or going down your throat. Other times they want the medicine to dissolve only when it has gotten all the way to your stomach. Medicines that are supposed to work for 8 or 12 hours need to take even longer to dissolve so the medicine will work all day long.

Stretch-O-Meter

If you want to shoot a rubber band really far, you stretch it as much as you can. Is there a way you can stretch it even farther?

?
How does temperature affect the stretch of a rubber band?

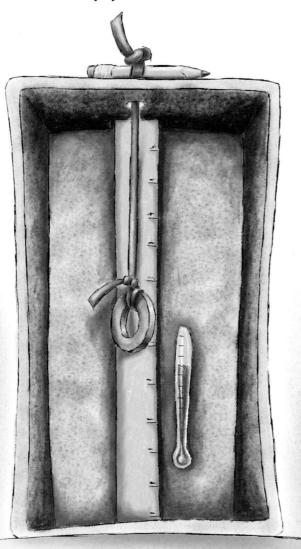

What You Need

- Shoebox
- Ruler
- Tape
- Thermometer
- Scissors
- Rubber band
- Washer
- Pencil
- Clock or stopwatch
- Refrigerator
- Hair dryer

Experiment

1 Find a shoebox long enough for the ruler to fit snugly inside. Tape the ruler to the bottom of the box. Tape the thermometer next to it.

2 Stand the shoebox on end. Poke a hole in the top of the box, in the middle.

3 Use the scissors to cut the rubber band so it's one long piece. Tie the washer to one end of the rubber band. Thread the other end through the hole.

4 Tie the rubber band to the middle of the pencil so that the weight on the other end can hang freely in the box. This is your Stretch-O-Meter!

5 Let the rubber band stretch for three minutes at room temperature. Write down the temperature on the thermometer. Measure and write down the length of the rubber band using the ruler in the Stretch-o-Meter.

6 Put the Stretch-o-Meter in the refrigerator for 15 minutes.

7 Open the refrigerator door. Write down the temperature on the thermometer. Measure and write down the length of the rubber band. Touch the rubber band. Write down how it feels.

8 Use the hair dryer to heat the rubber band in the Stretch-o-Meter for five minutes. Write down the temperature on the thermometer. Measure and write down the length of the rubber band. Touch the rubber band. Write down how it feels.

Conclusion

Make a line graph to show your results. Put the temperature on the **X** axis and the length of the rubber band on the **Y** axis. When did the rubber band have the most stretch? When did it have the least stretch? Is this what you expected?

> **Where can you find a rubber trumpet?**
>
> **In a rubber band!**

EXPLORE FURTHER

Take the temperature change to extremes by freezing and boiling the rubber band. (Have an adult help with this.) What happens if you use rubber bands of different sizes and shapes?

TAKE A CLOSER LOOK

Most things expand when they're heated, like the liquid in your thermometer or the air in a balloon. What happens to rubber when it's heated?

Rubber is a *polymer*. If you look at a polymer under a very strong microscope, you'll see long chains of molecules. When the rubber polymer is heated up, the chains start to wiggle and move around. Take a piece of long string and wiggle it back and forth on your desk. Does it look longer or shorter? When you cool the rubber polymer, the chains lie still. Are the chains longer or shorter when they're lying still?

Color Confusion

Test the eyesight of five of your friends with this colorful experiment.

?

How does color affect how well you can tell the difference between different shades?

What You Need

- 6 clear glasses or jars
- Masking tape
- Marker
- Water
- Measuring cup
- Food coloring (red, blue, and yellow)
- Spoon
- 5 or more volunteers

Experiment

1 Label the glasses A, B, C, D, E, and F with the masking tape and marker.

2 Fill the six glasses half full with water. Use the measuring cup to make sure you put the same amount of water in each glass.

3 Mix the glasses up so they're not in alphabetical order.

4 Put one drop of red food coloring in the first glass, two drops in the second glass and so on. Stir the food coloring into the water with the spoon. Write down how many drops of food coloring are in each glass.

5 Mix up the glasses. Then have your first volunteer come to the table. Ask her to put the shades of water in order from lightest to darkest. Write down what order she put the glasses in. Mix up the order of the glasses again.

6 Repeat step 5 with each volunteer.

7 Pour out the water in the glasses. Repeat steps 2 through 4, adding the blue food coloring to the water. Then repeat steps 5 and 6.

8 Repeat step 7 with the yellow food coloring.

Conclusion

For each color, compare the order your volunteers put the glasses in to the actual order (from step 4). Count how many glasses were out of order for each color. Which color had the most mistakes? Which had the fewest mistakes? Which shades of color do you think are easiest to tell apart? Which are the hardest?

EXPLORE FURTHER

What happens when you use other colors, such as orange, green, or purple? Time how long it takes the volunteers to put the shades in order. Do some colors take longer to order than others? Does the amount of water you use make it more or less difficult to tell the colors apart? What if you use milk instead of water? Does the type or amount of light affect how well we can order the colors? Try the experiment inside and outside, with fluorescent lights and incandescent lights, or with bright and dim lights.

TAKE A CLOSER LOOK

There are tiny *rods* and *cones* in the back of our eyeballs. This is how we see. The rods let us see black and white. The cones show us colors. The rods in our eyes work much better than the cones. Our eyes require bright light in order to see colors clearly. There are only three types of cones in our eyes. They see red, blue, and green. All the other colors we see are just a combination of these three colors. With these three types of cones we can tell apart about two million different shades of color!

People who are colorblind only have one or two types of cones in their eyeballs. They see everything as a combination of just one or two colors. This makes it harder to tell different colors apart.

What is green and red all over?

A pickle holding its breath!

Do You Feel That?

?

How does the place on your body affect how well your skin feels touch?

What's the biggest organ in your body? Your skin!

What You Need

- Scissors
- Ruler
- 5 different sizes of monofilament fishing line
- Tape
- 5 craft sticks
- Marker
- 5 or more volunteers
- Blindfold

Experiment

1. Cut a 2-inch (5.1 cm) piece of the thinnest fishing line and tape it to the craft stick so about 1½ inches (3.8 cm) hangs off the end of the stick. Use the marker to label the stick with the size of the fishing line.

2. Repeat step 1 for all the other sizes of fishing line.

3. Make a data table to record your data. Write the sizes of the fishing line across the top of the page and list the body parts you'll test down the left side: index fingertip, palm, back of hand, outside forearm, inside forearm, cheek, back of neck, front of neck, inside elbow, back of elbow, top of leg, and back of leg. Make a table for each of your volunteers.

4 Have each volunteer wear shorts and a short-sleeved shirt. Make sure that you test all the volunteers on the same day since a change in humidity can affect the size of the fishing line.

5 Blindfold your first volunteer. Have her place one hand on the table, palm up.

6 Hold the stick with the thinnest fishing line over the volunteer's index finger. Carefully lay the fishing line on the fingertip so that it bends slightly.

7 Ask the volunteer if she feels it. Mark "yes" or "no" on the data table.

What did one hand say to the other? Keep in touch!

8 Repeat steps 6 and 7 for all the other body parts. Once you've finished all the body parts, move on to the next thickness of fishing line. Go through all the body parts again. Do this for all the sizes of fishing line.

9 Repeat steps 5 through 8 for the rest of your volunteers.

Conclusion

Make a bar graph to show the results for each volunteer. Put the body parts on the X axis and the sizes of fishing line on the Y axis. Compare the graphs for each of your volunteers. Which body parts are the most sensitive? Which body parts are the least sensitive? Can you think of some reasons why some parts are more sensitive than others? Think about what we use different parts of our bodies for.

EXPLORE FURTHER

Does temperature affect how sensitive our skin is? Try the experiment outside on a cold day or see if you can try it in a sauna. What about different times of day? Are we more sensitive in the morning, afternoon, or evening?

TAKE A CLOSER LOOK

The parts of our skin that are most sensitive have more *receptors*, or touch detectors. These receptors can sense touch, temperature, and pressure just like a taste bud senses taste.

Your touch receptors keep you safe. If you feel something hot, it hurts so your body knows to move before you burn yourself.

More than 100 years ago, Max von Frey invented a tool to measure how sensitive our skin is to touch. Instead of fishing line, he used human, horse, pig, and goat hairs. These hairs are different thicknesses, just like the fishing line you used. Aren't you glad you didn't have to pluck hairs off a pig to do your experiment?

Spin City

Raise your spin-telligence with this experiment.

?

How does the weight on a whirly gig affect how long it takes to fall?

What You Need

- Whirligig template
- Paper
- Pencil
- Scissors
- Chair
- Yardstick or meterstick
- Stopwatch
- Paper clips

Experiment

1. Carefully trace the whirligig template to the left onto a piece of paper and cut it out. Don't cut on the dotted line. Fold one of the top flaps forward and the other backward.

2. Stand on a chair and hold the whirligig so it's 2 yards (2 m) high. Drop your whirligig. How does it fall? Write down what you see.

3 Drop the whirligig from 2 yards (2 m) high again and use the stopwatch to time how long it takes to hit the ground. Write down the time.

4 Repeat step 3 four more times.

5 Put a paper clip on the bottom of the whirly gig. Repeat steps 2 through 4.

6 Repeat steps 2 through 4 with two paper clips.

7 Keep adding paper clips and repeating steps 2 through 4 until you can't fit any more on the bottom or until you run out of paper clips.

Conclusion

For each number of paper clips, calculate the average time it took the whirligig to fall (see page 9). Make a line graph to show your results. Put the number of paper clips on the **X** axis and the average fall time on the **Y** axis. How many paper clips could you fit on the whirligig? How did this change the time it took to fall?

EXPLORE FURTHER

You can change the shape and size of the whirligig or where you place the paper clips. See how this affects the time it takes to fall. Test how accurate the whirligig is. Make a target for the whirligig and count how many times you hit the bull's eye. What happens when you drop it from different heights or go outside when it's windy?

TAKE A CLOSER LOOK

Have you seen the seeds from maple trees spinning to the ground in the spring? Maple seeds need to fall as slowly as possible so they can get far away from the tree. If they're far away from the tree, they'll have more sunshine to help them grow. As they spin and float through the air, hopefully they'll catch a breeze that will carry them off to a nice sunny spot. The maple seed is shaped just like your whirligig. The heavy seed at the bottom is like the paper clip on your whirligig. The wings are at the top of both.

Whirligigs and maple seeds are called *autorotators*. This means they start to spin when they fall. The wings at the top let the whirly gig catch the air and float. The paper clip at the bottom pulls the whirligig down. These two forces, on opposite ends of the whirligig, make it spin.

What did the washer say to the dryer?

I'll give it a whirl.

Glossary

Absorb. To soak up.

Abstract. A brief summary of the main parts of a paper.

Autorotator. An object that spins as it falls.

Auxin. A chemical that helps plants grow roots.

Average. A single number that represents many other numbers.

Bar graph. A graph that uses rectangles to show the relationship between two things.

Colloid. A mixture that acts like both a liquid and a solid.

Condensation. The change that occurs when a gas turns into a liquid.

Cones. The cone-shaped cells in the back of our eyes that see color.

Control. The part of the experiment that doesn't change.

Data. The measurements and observations you gather.

Data table. The table where you write down all your data.

Dependent variable. Something that is affected when you change the independent variable.

Digest. To break down a substance (usually food) into smaller particles that can be absorbed.

Dissolve. To be absorbed by a liquid.

Enzyme. A chemical that makes a change happen in a living organism. For example, some enzymes help fruit grow and ripen. Other enzymes digest food.

Epithelial olfactory receptor. A receptor cell in your nose that detects smells.

Evaporation. The change that occurs when a liquid turns into a gas.

Force. The strength of a push or a pull.

Gluten. A protein found in wheat, corn, and some other grains.

Gravity. The force that makes objects move toward the center of the earth.

Hypothesis. Your guess about what you think you'll find out with your experiment.

Independent variable. The thing you change in an experiment.

Iris. The colored part of the eye.

Line graph. A graph that uses lines to show the relationship between two things.

Melanin. A dark pigment that affects the color of hair, eyes, and skin.

Meniscus. The curve around the edges of a liquid held in a container.

Mineral. The stuff rocks are made of.

Mordant. A substance that makes dye permanent.

Mucus. The slippery, sticky liquid found in your nose and mouth.

Outlier. A measurement or result that does not fit with the rest of the data collected.

Polymer. A substance made of many molecules linked together in a chain.

Protein. A substance that is the basis of all living things and is essential for life.

Pupil. The opening in the iris that lets light through.

Receptor. A special cell in your body that detects smell, taste, light, or touch.

Reflect. To throw back or give an image of.

Retina. The surface on the back of the eye that senses light and forms an image.

Rods. The rod-shaped cells in the back of our eyes that see black and white.

Scientific method. The plan scientists use to answer questions.

Supersaturated solution. A mixture of liquid and a dissolved solid that is so full of the solid it can't hold any more.

Trial. The taking of a measurement (or set of measurements). Trials are repeated many times in an experiment.

Viscosity. The degree to which a substance can flow.

X axis. The horizontal line on the bottom of a bar or line graph.

Y axis. The vertical line on the side of a bar or line graph.

Acknowledgments

Thanks to everyone who made this book possible, especially:

My assistants, Geoff and Sam, who helped out with the science projects all over the house.

Cindy Lickert, who made sure that kids will enjoy reading this book (and for always being a good friend!).

Gina Barrier, who helped me keep safety first.

Jenny Mercer, who shared her insight into the working of a child's mind.

Lily Roman, who field tested the Exploding Soda project and reminded me how much fun 10 year olds have with science.

My editor, Rain Newcomb, who I couldn't have done this book without.

Nora Thompson, who filled this book with beautiful illustrations.

Erik Johnson, who helped write some of the jokes.

Index